ABSOLUTELY CONKERS

ABSOLUTELY CONKERS

Ian Cooper

The Book Guild Ltd
Sussex, England

The Book Guild Ltd
25 High Street,
Lewes, Sussex

First published 1998

Set in Souvenir Light

Typesetting by Wordset
Hassocks, West Sussex

Printed in Great Britain by
Bookcraft (Bath) Ltd. Avon

A catalogue record for this book is
available from the British Library

ISBN 1 85776 293 2

For Minx,
Paul and Mark

The small picturesque village of Ashton, in Northamptonshire, is the setting for the World Conker Championships. Competitors for this annual event travel from far and wide, along with thousands of spectators who gather to watch the clashing of conkers. It is upon this typically English tradition that this book is based.

1

Mr Sponge, the school caretaker, was not a happy man. He was cleaning Class 5R.

'Conkers! Conkers! Conkers! If I see another conker I shall go absolutely –'

'Nuts, Mr Sponge?'

'Oh, good afternoon, Headmaster. I'm glad you're here. Just look at this room. Look at it. It's a disgrace. There's conkers everywhere. Have you seen the mess on the carpet? There's conker shells under every desk. There's even a conker in the model of the Viking longboat. It's like this every time I come in here.'

'Yes, I know just what you mean, Mr Sponge. I'm afraid that this conker business is getting a bit out of hand. Why, only this morning as I was driving to school, I had to swerve to avoid being hit by a large piece of wood. Some children were throwing sticks into a tree trying to knock the conkers down.' The headmaster stood with his arms folded trying to look sympathetic.

Although he was very concerned about the problems created by the conker craze, the headmaster was secretly hoping that this latest children's fad would soon come to an end, particularly as autumn was fast drawing to a close. He stood thinking about the games that he used to play when he was at school. Marbles was his favourite, where he often won 'Chinas' and 'Spaghettis', and once even a 'King Kong'. Then there was 'Clackers', those two plastic balls on the end of a piece of string. They were really great, and you could –.

'I said perhaps we could do something about it then, headmaster?'

'What? Oh yes. Certainly, Mr Sponge. I'll speak to the teachers tomorrow.'

The headmaster turned and walked back towards his office, trying to remember where he'd stored his old school things. Perhaps he could get them out sometime and have a quick game or two with them.

At the following morning's staff meeting Mr North, the headmaster, was feeling pretty pleased with himself. The previous evening he'd played his wife at marbles and had beaten her by two games to one. Safe and happy in the knowledge that he was still the champion marble player in his own household, he settled down to open the meeting.

'Now then, ladies and gentlemen,' the headmaster began. 'Mr Sponge informs me that some boys and girls are causing a few problems with conkers.'

'They certainly are!' a stern voice immediately responded. The voice belonged to Miss Stoat, a large, fierce woman who looked at least 75 years old. She had a bushy mop of grey hair knotted tightly in a bun on the top of her rectangular head. She always agreed with the headmaster. No one ever disagreed with Miss Stoat.

'Er, yes, thank you, Miss Stoat,' said Mr North.

'I agree,' said Mr Smith, who was new to the school and was trying extremely hard to impress Miss Stoat.

'Well,' said the headmaster, 'I have given the problem a great deal of thought,' which actually

meant that he'd had an idea as he was driving through the school gate earlier that morning. 'What I suggest is that we organise some sort of tournament amongst the children. It would be a sort of end of the conker season challenge competition. Then, when it was over, we wouldn't allow any more conker contests on the school premises.'

'Splendid idea!' boomed Miss Stoat immediately the headmaster paused for breath.

'Does anyone have any objections' asked the headmaster as he examined his knuckles, which he'd bruised during last night's marbles match. 'Jolly good! Shall we say next weekend then?'

The headmaster was delighted with his planning. That was the weekend of the headmasters' conference, so he wouldn't be able to attend the conker tournament and risk the embarrassment of being beaten by one of the children.

'I shall leave the competition in the capable hands of our very own sports fanatic, Mr Leaton, and I hope that as many of you as possible will attend. Is that okay, Mr Leaton?'

'Ah, well, um, er,' stuttered Mr Leaton, trying to avoid the glare of Miss Stoat, and the delighted glances of the other members of staff, who were only too pleased at not being given another weekend task to complete.

'Good? That's settled then. I'll invite Mr Sponge along to help you. Just one other item,' the headmaster continued, 'a reminder to the music teacher, Miss Note, that there is a birthday on Friday, so we shall require a "Happy Birthday" to be played during the assembly. Well, that's all for now. Let's have a super day.' The headmaster rose and marched quickly out of the room, trying to avoid any awkward questions that may be posed at such an early hour of the morning.

Mr Leaton was a tall, athletic-looking teacher who was popular with the children. He always wore a tracksuit to school, much to the annoyance of Miss Stoat, and he would often stop and join in the children's games, much to the annoyance of Mr North. He now sat in a daze as the other members of staff immediately offered him their regrets that unfortunately they would be unable to offer him any help with the tournament due to urgent appointments and visiting sick relatives. All that is, except for Miss Stoat, who proudly announced in a loud voice that she'd be travelling with the headmaster, in order to help him prepare for the conference.

Unfortunately, Mr Leaton had also arranged his weekend's entertainment, which involved his new sports car and trying to impress a pretty young lady by the name of Rosalind. It appeared that these carefully made plans would now have to be altered, a fact which did not please him one little bit. It was, therefore, a very unhappy Mr Leaton who walked towards Class 5R for the English language lesson. If he heard just one word about conkers . . . !

The boys of 5R were waiting noisily outside their classroom. They couldn't understand why 'Sporty' Leaton, as they'd secretly nicknamed him, was late. However, they did know that the later he was, the less English they'd have to do. But at this moment in time, the children had other things on their minds, because Badger Watts and Joey Roberts were arguing over the best way to harden conkers.

'It's lemon juice,' insisted Badger, a large plump

child whose real name was Ian. He was the class joker, and if anyone was going to get into trouble, it was Badger. In fact, he didn't need to look for trouble, because it always found him.

'Put 'em in the oven,' insisted Joey, a curly-haired stick of a lad. The two boys were really the best of friends, but since this conker craze had started they were both desperately keen to be the best player in the school. This had led to many arguments.

'Soak 'em in lemon juice.'

'Nah, put them in the oven.'

'Lemon juice.'

'In the oven.'

'Lemon juice.'

'Right, quiet you lot.' Mr Leaton had arrived, and it was obvious that he was not his usual happy self. Immediately the children entered the classroom, they were set to work, and Mr Leaton launched into a tirade of how to use sentences correctly. Unfortunately, Badger and Joey were both determined to have the last word, and were whispering to each other.

'It's lemon juice.'

'In the oven.'

'Lemon juice.'

'In the oven.'

The already annoyed teacher detected that two boys were not paying full attention, and he fired a quick question, pointing at Badger as he did so.

'What goes at the end of a sentence?'

Badger, quite unprepared, immediately replied, 'Lemon juice.'

The class roared with laughter, and Mr Leaton was quite taken aback, until he remembered his own schooldays. The only use that he knew for lemon juice was to harden conkers!

The explosion that followed did not last a particularly long time, but it was quite apparent that the teacher, at this particular moment, was not too fond of conkers. Indeed, after the forthcoming competition he did not expect to hear another word on the subject, ever again. Unfortunately, Mr Leaton had not intended to let the children of 5R know about the competition. He figured that the fewer the people who knew about it, the fewer the people who would turn up for it. In fact it might even have to be cancelled. However, during his verbal bashing of the children, he had inadvertently let slip a few important words. His mistake was immediately noticed by Badger and Joey, who were already asking themselves questions as they left the classroom at the end of the lesson, complete with the extra work that their teacher had set them for not paying attention.

'What did he mean "school competition"?' quizzed Joey.

'How do I know?' Badger replied, 'but I think we should find out.'

'How shall we do that? I'm not asking him. At least not while he's in this mood,' Joey added.

'Don't worry, he won't be like that for long. I'll ask him at lunchtime. I expect he'll come and join in whatever we're playing.'

'Well, make sure you don't forget,' said Joey, anxious to make sure that he got all the details.

'I will, you'll see,' answered Badger. 'Come on, I'm starving. Let's see what I've got for snack,' and he walked off to fetch his sandwich box.

2

The morning of the school conker competition was bright and breezy. It was an ideal day for a nice drive in the country, especially if you had an attractive young lady as a passenger. This was exactly what Mr Leaton was thinking as he drove towards the school to organise the tournament. He had spent the remainder of the previous week avoiding questions from children about the competition. In fact, apart from one or two persistent boys – most notably Badger and Joey – he had managed to keep details of the tournament extremely quiet. Other members of the staff had also forgotten to mention the tournament, in case they were asked to come along and help out. The only person to discuss the event with Mr Leaton was Miss Take, the school secretary. After being told to keep her voice down, she was immediately elected as the official judge. This was rather unfortunate for her, as she had only gone to speak to Mr Leaton to inform him that on the day of the contest Jennifer Morgan was having her birthday party, and all the girls in the school were invited, but definitely no boys! This didn't bother the boys, however, because one of the local youth clubs had organised a coach trip to see the big football match, and nearly all of them would be going to that. These alternative activities fitted in well with Mr Leaton's plans. With a bit of luck there'd be so few children turning up for his competition that he'd be back home for lunch. This would give him just about enough time to have a quick snack before his relaxing afternoon drive with Rosalind. It was with these pleasant thoughts in mind that he pulled into the school car park.

Badger and Joey had been waiting in the school playground since eight o'clock, a full hour before the contest was due to start. It was now almost nine o'clock, and the only other person that they had seen was Miss Take, the school secretary. It appeared that she was wearing a blonde curly wig and a baggy red sack!

'I told you that it was stupid having the competition today,' said Badger.

'No it's not, there'll be more people than this turning up. You'll see,' Joey replied.

'Hey look, here's Sporty Leaton coming.'

Mr Leaton got out of his posh new sports car and walked towards the boys.

'Hello, boys.'

'Hello, Spor – er Mr Leaton.'

'Where are the others then?'

'I don't think there are any others, Mr Leaton. I think most people have gone on the trip, or have gone to Jennifer's birthday party. Either that or they've forgotten.'

'Oh well, never mind, boys,' Mr Leaton replied, working out how long it would take him to get home. Perhaps he would even have time to stop off at the florist's and buy some flowers for Rosalind.

'It's a bit of a waste of time, Mr Leaton,' said Badger, looking down in the dumps. 'I can't understand it. *Some* of our class said that they were coming – Glen, Neil, Robin, Geoff, they all said they'd be here.'

Mr Leaton began to have feelings of guilt. Perhaps he should have mentioned the competition a bit more often. He could see that pretty soon he was going to have two depressed boys on his hands, and he had to act quickly to cheer them up.

'I'm sure that some others will turn up. Look, here's someone now.'

A small blonde girl strolled up, wearing a blue tee shirt with patterned stains of yesterday's beans on toast splattered on its front.

'Uh, it's only Soppy Susan,' said the boys together. 'I wonder what she wants.'

'Hello, Susan,' said Mr Leaton. 'I'm glad you could come.'

'Oh, I've only come to get my lunch box,' giggled Susan. 'I left it behind yesterday. Can I fetch it please?'

'Huh! So much for another competitor,' the boys whispered to each other.

'Yes you can, Susan. Off you go.'

Mr Leaton began to feel a little worried. What would Miss Stoat and the headmaster say when they heard that only two people had turned up for his tournament? He tried to put on a brave face.

'Well, boys, don't worry. We'll still have a great competition,' he said, feeling more downhearted by the minute. 'Look, there's us three, Miss Take and Mr Sponge,' he continued, trying to sound enthusiastic. 'Where is Mr Sponge? Have you seen him, boys?'

At that moment, Miss Take, looking slightly flustered and definitely odd in her flowing red gown rushed from the warmth of her office, out into the playground. She had been relaxing with a large mug of decaffeinated coffee, which she had purposely made in Miss Stoat's expensive china mug.

'Mr Leaton! Mr Leaton!' exclaimed Miss Take as she dashed across the playground, splashing coffee from the mug.

'Yes, Miss Take, what's the matter? Why are you dressed –'

'That was Mr Sponge on the telephone,' she interrupted. 'I'm afraid he won't be coming this morning. He's had to take his cat, Tiddles, to the vet. It's an emergency.'

Miss Take, being an animal lover, sounded genuinely concerned.

'This gets worse and worse,' moaned Badger.

'Oh dear,' said Mr Leaton, who had also come into contact with a few pussy cats – mainly when he was driving his car! 'Did he say what happened?'

'Yes, Mr Leaton. He said that he had a problem with his washing machine.'

'So he's gone to the vet's?' asked Mr Leaton, slightly puzzled. 'Whatever do you mean, Miss Take?'

'Well, the washing machine wouldn't work until he closed the door and pressed the "on" button.'

'So did he do that?'

'Yes, Mr Leaton.'

'And what happened . . . did it work?'

'Yes, Mr Leaton. It worked really well.'

'So what is the problem, Miss Take?' asked the frustrated teacher.

'Well, Tiddles was asleep in it at the time.'

'Oh dear. Poor pussy,' said a concerned Mr Leaton, thinking how he'd feel if he was shut in a small metal box with a pair of Mr Sponge's socks. 'Yes, Joey, what is it?'

'Could we say that there's been a catastrophe, Mr Leaton?'

'Oh yes, Joey, very funny, most amusing. Now then, are we going to get this competition on the move?' Mr Leaton was trying to put together some sort of contest out of the remains of what was turning out to be a pretty disastrous day for everyone. 'Come along, boys. I'm sure that Miss Take will join us. That will make four entrants altogether.'

'Big deal,' muttered Badger to himself.

'Oh but Mr Leaton,' said Miss Take, 'I can't play conkers. I've never played before, and I don't know anything about them. Anyway, I'm only the judge, that's why I wore these clothes.'

Badger and Joey twisted their faces as they tried not to laugh at Miss Take's outfit.

'Nonsense, Miss Take. Anyone can play conkers. I tell you what, I'll be the judge of your game and see that there's fair play. Now then, where's your conker?'

'But I don't have one.'

Another obstacle was placed in Mr Leaton's path.

'Oh but . . . oh well, I'm sure that the boys will have a spare. Badger?'

'No, Mr Leaton. I've only got my best conker.'

Now this was not strictly true, because Badger did have a spare conker. In fact, he had two pocketfuls of spare conkers, but he did not intend to give his potential opponent a chance of beating him using one of his own conkers. As far as he was concerned, if you didn't have your own conker you were out of the competition.

'Oh dear. Joey, do you have a spare conker that Miss Take could borrow?'

Joey's hands immediately curled around a small

bag that he was holding. He hoped that the brown crinkled paper wouldn't be seen.

'Just one, Joey. Anything will do, really.'

Joey was of the same opinion of competitions as Badger. If you entered a tournament, you should supply your own conker. However, realising that Mr Leaton may have seen him covering his bag, he admitted that he may just have a small spare nut.

'Good lad, Joey,' said Mr Leaton with a sigh of relief. At long last his tournament was under way.

Joey's hand dipped into his crumpled bag and pulled out Miss Take's conker, which resembled a mouldy frozen pea with a large crack down one side.

'Sorry, Mr Leaton, but it's the only spare that I have with me,' said Joey, who sensed that any of the conkers that he had in his bag would be able to beat the small shrivelled nut that he now handed to Mr Leaton.

'Good, we're all set. Now, as we only have three conkers, only three people can play. So, I propose that Miss Take and Joey play off, with the winner playing Badger in the final.'

Badger immediately cheered up. He could see a chance of becoming school conker champion by only playing one match. Similarly, Joey was quite pleased because he would have the chance to practise his 'super smash swing' on Miss Take's shrivelled pea.

'Right then, boys, er, and Miss Take, the rules are as follows. Each person takes turns at having three hits, and we carry on until one of the conkers breaks. All clear? Oh, I almost forgot, no tangling strings, and no stamps. Are we ready?'

'Er, Mr Leaton,' said Miss Take rather nervously. 'What are stamps?'

Badger gazed into the air and muttered to himself

under his breath.

'Well, Miss Take, it means that if your opponent's conker falls onto the floor, you're not allowed to stamp on it.'

'Oh dear, I should hope not,' stated Miss Take, who was beginning to look rather pale.

'Okay then. Off we go,' Mr Leaton enthused. 'Joey and Miss Take is the first event.'

Joey pulled out a smooth, polished brown conker that was neatly threaded onto a black football bootlace. It was the size of a golf ball. This nut was the pride of his collection as it had already beaten eight other conkers, making it an 'eighter'. Miss Take held a small yellow-green shrivelled pea in the sweaty palm of her nervous hand.

'Er, Miss Take, you haven't threaded your conker.'

'Oh. Do I need to?'

Badger and Joey were both now covering their faces and pretending to cough. It was the only way that they could stop themselves from bursting into laughter. Mr Leaton, sensing a breakdown in his fast-improving competition, immediately bent down and removed a short brown lace from his new Italian-design moccasin shoes, which he had bought especially for this weekend. He reached forward and took Miss Take's small wrinkled conker and proceeded to slip the lace between the large crack until it held firm. Miss Take put her coffee down on the step by her feet and took the swinging nut from the teacher.

'Right, all set?' asked Mr Leaton. 'Miss Take, you can take the first hit.'

Miss Take took a hesitant step forward and faced a relaxed Joey, who was holding his huge gleaming conker out at arm's length.

Miss Take gritted her teeth, stood bolt upright, clenched her muscles tight, pulled back her conker and swung with all her might. The small frizzled conker shot off the brown lace and headed towards Joey, who, seeing a yellow brown ball hurtling towards him, dropped his conker and covered his face with his hands to protect himself. Miss Take, seeing Joey's hands rushing upwards, immediately lunged backwards, knocking into Mr Leaton. As she struggled to stop herself from falling over, her tall pointed heel stepped onto a large shiny conker that had just fallen onto the floor.

'My conker!' shouted Joey, as a loud crack was followed by the soft dull scraping of heel on nut. Miss Take looked down at Joey's flattened sphere crushed beneath her heel.

'You said "no stamps", he cried to Mr Leaton. 'You said "no stamps".'

Mr Leaton was not listening. He was too busy picking himself up from the step onto which he had fallen when Miss Take had barged into him. Worse still was that he had actually landed on Miss Stoat's china coffee mug, which now lay in a hundred tiny pieces in a puddle of cold coffee at his feet.

'I won! I won!' shouted Miss Take.

'No stamps!' retorted Joey.

'Mr Leaton, Mr Leaton, I won, didn't I? I won, Mr Leaton.'

Sporty Leaton wasn't really bothered about who won or lost, at this precise moment. All he could think of was how to explain a broken mug to Miss Stoat, and that he now had a cold, wet, coffee-covered foot in an unlaced new shoe.

'Mr Leaton, I'm in the final, aren't I?' Miss Take persevered.

'Oh yes! If you must be,' stormed Sporty, trying to remain calm.

'But that's not fair!' pleaded Joey. 'You said "no stamps".'

By now Mr Leaton had lost all interest in the competition.

'Oh be quiet, Joey. It was an accident, it doesn't matter.'

'But you said "no stamps"!' Joey pleaded. He looked as if he was about to burst into tears.

'Please, Mr Leaton, someone threw this small pea

at me as I was coming back from fetching my lunch box.' It was Susan, who had nearly been blinded by the small conker hurtling towards her as she was walking across the playground towards the school gate.

'Oh thank you, thank you Susan,' said Miss Take. 'I wondered where it had gone.' Miss Take picked the conker from Susan's gleaming white palm and began to dance in small steps, singing 'My conker's a oner! My conker's a oner!' as she did so.

'I say, Mr Leaton,' said Susan, 'you don't look too well. Are you all right?'

'I was!' snapped Mr Leaton.

'Oh dear,' continued Susan in a concerned voice, 'isn't that the mug that Miss Stoat uses?'

'Oh please go home Susan, we're in the middle of an important competition,' Mr Leaton replied in a less than friendly voice.

Badger, who had been watching the events with a look of amazement and disbelief, was now trying to console his friend. He agreed that the contest was unfair and that the result shouldn't be allowed to stand. However, judging by Mr Leaton's current mood, it didn't seem too wise to broach the subject with his teacher. Badger therefore confidently assured his pal that he would thrash silly old Miss Take's conker in the final.

'But that means you'll be the conker champion of the school,' gulped Joey. 'That's not fair!'

Indeed it did mean that, thought Badger.

Although becoming the school conker champion was his ultimate aim, Badger would have preferred it to come about in far more pleasant circumstances than this. He reached into his pocket and pulled out a handful of conkers, most of which were already threaded onto laces. He selected a lace with a small piece of yellow cotton tied to it. This identified his prize conker – a twelver!

'Right, come on then, Badger,' boomed Mr Leaton, as he squelched noisily towards the two contestants in his wet shoe. 'Let's have the final and then we can all go home and relax. Miss Take, bearing in mind the chaos caused by yourself in the first game, I suggest that Badger has first hit.'

'Alright, Mr Leaton, but tell him to be gentle.'

'Right, off you go, Badger. Wait!!!! Let me stand back and well out of the way, I'd do the same if I were you, Joey.'

Joey moodily retreated to a safe distance.

Miss Take grimaced, screwed her face up tightly and clenched each and every muscle in her body. She stood rigid with limbs locked, dangling her cracked conker at arm's length. In front of her, Badger, slightly nervous, set himself up for the first strike.

I'll make it a good one, he thought to himself. With that, he pulled hard down on his taut string and waited to hear the sharp crack as the nuts collided.

Silence.

Unbelievably, Badger had missed with his first shot.

Yeeeeeaaaahhhhhh!!!! cried Miss Take when she noticed that her nut was still suspended on the brown lace.

However, a split second later, the sudden draught of air caused by Badger's moving missile pushed against Miss Take's conker, which moved slightly in the gentle breeze and then dropped into two halves onto the playground.

'That's not fair!' wailed Miss Take.

'Does that count, Mr Leaton?' asked a surprised Badger.

Mr Leaton, wet-footed, annoyed and in a desperate hurry to get home and forget all about the morning's unfortunate events, did not really care whether gusts of air should be allowed to affect conker competition results or not.

'It doesn't say anything in the rules that the conkers *must* hit each other,' he said. 'So I declare Badger Watts the school conker champion.'

'Oh but Mr Leaton,' wailed Miss Take, 'Badger made too much wind.'

'Not now, Miss Take. Badger has won fair and square.'

In fact, Mr Leaton was quite relieved that one of the boys had won. It would help to cheer them up after what, it must be admitted, was a disappointing tournament.

'Right, boys, well done for taking part, and congratulations, Badger. I'll tell Mr North the result on Monday. Off you go now and Miss Take and I will clear up and make sure that all the doors and windows are locked. 'Bye now.' Mr Leaton rattled off his words in double quick time. He was so relieved that this bizarre competition had at last come to an end. Perhaps now he could head off home, prepare for a relaxing afternoon's drive with his lady friend and enjoy the rest of the weekend.

'Looks like Miss Take has already left, Mr Leaton,' said Badger. 'Look, she's just getting into her car now.'

'Pardon? Oh yes, er, she must be in a hurry. Thank you, Badger,' said the boys' teacher as he watched Miss Take slam her car door and drive moodily away, screeching the car tyres as she did so. 'You and Joey should be getting yourselves off home now as well.'

'Yes, okay,' replied Badger. 'Hmm, Mr Leaton,' he

continued, 'was there a prize for winning the competition?'

Arrgh! Mr Leaton thought to himself. Not only had he failed to tell anyone about the competition, but he had also forgotten all about a prize.

'A prize?' said Mr Leaton in a loud voice. 'Er, of course there's a prize.'

'Oh thanks, Mr Leaton,' answered the school champion, watched by an inquisitive Joey standing beside him. 'What is it?'

'W-What is it?' stuttered the teacher.

'Yes, Mr Leaton,' said Badger.

'Well, it's um, er . . . You want to know what your prize is?'

'Yes please!'

'Well, it's er, er something different. Something *very* different.'

'Oh great,' said Badger. 'So what is it, Mr Leaton?'

'Well it's a, er, um a surprise!'

'Oh great! I love surprises. Can Joey share it with me?' asked Badger.

'Er, well, we'll see later, shall we? I really must be getting off now, boys. I have a very urgent meeting to attend.'

Mr Leaton was getting more flustered by the minute. This morning seemed to be one problem after another.

'Okay, thanks, Mr Leaton. But when do we get this surprise?' inquired Badger.

'Oh yes, um, well er, first thing on Monday morning, boys. During the school assembly.'

'Oh thanks, Mr Leaton,' replied a delighted Badger. 'Come on, Joey, let's go down to the market and see if there's anything happening there.'

'Okay,' said Joey, who was feeling slightly happier,

since it didn't appear as if Badger was going to brag about winning the competition.

'Right. 'Bye then, boys.'

''Bye, Mr Leaton,' echoed the boys as they strolled towards the school gates.

As Sporty Leaton drove home after the competition, he was deep in worried thought. Not only had he to explain to Miss Stoat how he had broken her best china coffee mug, but he also had to think of a suitable prize to give to Badger for winning the tournament. In addition, the prize had to be different, something *very* different.

'Whatever can I get?' he said to himself. 'Whatever can I get?'

3

The small town of Grizzleby was usually a quiet, relaxed neighbourhood, where elderly women stopped and talked about the weather. Their husbands would sit on green wooden benches and discuss the latest rise in the price of a pint of beer, whilst small children played happily in the narrow alleyways that ran between the terraced houses.

But not on Saturdays.

For on Saturdays, the sleepy little town came alive. The dreary, relaxed pace of the previous six days was lost amongst the hustle and bustle of the market. There was a tremendous buzz of excitement, and a hive of activity as tradesmen travelled from all over the country to sell their goods. It was reputed that you could buy anything and everything you ever wanted on the Grizzleby stalls, from a left-handed mug to a second-hand stamp-licking machine.

Due to its size, the market attracted huge crowds of shoppers. They came from miles around and weaved their way methodically through the maze of stalls, buying all manner of strange objects. Particularly popular with the shoppers were the fruit and vegetable stalls. These always seemed to have some new weird and wonderful fruits on display, imported from some faraway exotic country.

It was on one such stall that Harry Sprout worked. He was a short, plump man with straight dark hair, and when he wasn't looking at the large gold rings

H. SPROUT
RESH FRUIT
VEGETABLES

that he had on each of his stubby fingers, he was picking the dirt from beneath his nails. Harry Sprout didn't try very hard to sell his fruit and vegetables. In fact, a careful look at Harry's stall would reveal that much of his produce was quite past its best, being only suitable for school dinners. The reason that Harry didn't care for selling his produce was that he had another way of making money. A very naughty way! Harry Sprout could arrange to buy and sell *anything*. His speciality was importing goods from overseas – with no questions asked. This contraband would be hidden away amongst the fresh fruit and vegetables that arrived daily from almost anywhere in the world. Harry could have something delivered to you before you could say 'how much'.

'How much?' said a small grey-haired old lady, pointing to a wrinkled, soft red-brown object.

'Pardon?'

'How much for the wrinkled red grapes?' she tried again.

'They're not grapes, they're plums!' Harry corrected the customer. 'They're best quality, just a little old.'

'They don't look much like plums to me,' said the woman, who had never previously mixed up her fruits. 'Haven't you got any grapes?'

'No I haven't,' said Harry. In fact, this is all I've got and you wouldn't like them, so if I were you I'd go to another stall!'

Harry was more abrupt than usual, mainly because he was expecting a visitor.

'But young man,' the woman continued, blocking the narrow path that ran between the stalls, 'I need some red grapes for my cough. I've had it for some time. I'm eighty-two, you know.'

'Madam, I don't think that these grapes, er, plums are the answer to your cough. Now if you'll excuse me . . .'

'Er, Mr Sprout,' a voice said as a man appeared behind the woman, 'I'm sure you'll serve this lady with those wonderful "grapes". My treat,' and he gave a wink with his right eye.

'Oh no, I couldn't accept them,' said the elderly woman.

'No, I do insist. My friend, er rather, the assistant was rather rude to you just now. It's the least we could do,' the man said.

'Oh thank you,' said the woman. 'I'm eighty-two, you know.'

Harry Sprout filled a bag with the soft, wrinkled red 'grapes' and handed them over to the aged customer.

'Oh thank you again,' she said, 'I'll come back here next time.'

Uh, I hope not! Harry Sprout thought to himself.

The tall stranger who owned the voice placed a few coins on the wooden table top and smiled at the elderly lady revealing a set of shining white teeth. He wore a smart two-piece pinstripe suit along with a large red and blue spotted tie. It was the visitor that Harry was expecting. His name was Edward Stone, better known as 'Ed'.

'Hello, Ed,' said Harry. Did you know that's the first thing I've sold all morning?'

'I'm not surprised,' Ed replied in a sarcastic voice.

Ed Stone was a nasty piece of work. He was a tall slim man and he wore expensive-looking jewellery. His sharp shifty eyes gave him an evil look, which he often used to good effect.

'I see that you've got some nuts for sale,' Ed remarked, pointing to a small brown pyramid at the front of the stall. 'Are there any walnuts amongst them?'

'No, I'm afraid they haven't been delivered. Should be here in a couple of weeks. As soon as I get them I'll save them for you,' Harry replied.

'Good. I've been expecting them. I'll pick them up myself. Remember, I only want the "best quality" ones.' Ed appeared slightly nervous and he kept glancing over his left shoulder. He edged forward and leaned towards Harry, flashing his brilliant white teeth. 'I've been thinking,' he whispered, 'it's probably best if we pretend that we don't know each other when I come to collect them, to avoid suspicion. Don't use my name. Think of a code word or something.'

'Okay, Ed,' said Harry. 'You know you can rely on me.'

Ed had a final look over his shoulder and said in a deep, menacing voice, 'Remember, only the "best quality". Two weeks.'

'I'll remember,' Harry replied. 'Cause you're paying me a lot of money! Oooopps.' He looked around to see if anyone had heard his last statement, and then turned back to face Ed. He was too late. Mr Stone had gone. He'd vanished into the crowd of Saturday shoppers. Harry had a quick look around his stall just to check there were no suspicious characters about, and then he went back to picking out a particularly stubborn piece of dirt from beneath his left thumbnail.

4

Monday morning had arrived far to quickly for Sporty Leaton. He'd had a pleasant weekend showing off to his lady friend in his fast new sports car, and he had quite forgotten about the prizes for the conker competition. Indeed, it was only when a large soggy cornflake had fallen from his spoon onto the morning newspaper as he was eating his breakfast cereal, that he was reminded of his dilemma. The cornflake had landed on a photograph of a large bald-headed man holding a conker. Beneath the picture the caption read 'Ivor Nutt to Retire!' Sporty scooped up the soggy orange flake and popped it into his mouth, reading over the article that appeared below the photograph as he did so. The article was a short piece and said:

> Mr Ivor Nutt, last year's world conker champion, has decided to retire. Mr Nutt said that despite entering this year's tournament he would not be taking part. He'd had a smashing time last year, and had managed to 'conquer' the world. He would now be happy to let someone else win the championship. The organisers of the competition said that they were disappointed that Mr Nutt had decided to retire, but understood his reasons for doing so. They would now have to find a suitable substitute competitor to replace him.

Arthur Leaton sat for a moment and then a feeling of panic came over him as he realized that in a very

short time the whole school would be expecting him to announce a suitable prize for winning the school competition. But then a large grin came on his face.

'Yeeesssss! I've got it! I've got it! Yaahhey!!' He stood up in his Tom and Jerry pyjamas, and danced a few steps around his small cramped kitchen. He was seen only by the local postman, who was passing the window as he delivered the morning mail.

Sporty Leaton left for school immediately, and he arrived earlier than he had ever done during the whole of his teaching career. This was immediately noticed by the other members of staff, who enquired if his house had burned down. The teachers also noticed that not only was Mr Leaton in an exceedingly good mood, but since arriving at school he'd been on the telephone virtually the whole time, making at least three long-distance calls. Finally, after telling Miss Stoat how well she looked, and buying four books of her raffle tickets, Mr Leaton stood in the centre of the staff room in order to make an announcement. He cleared his throat and then proudly told the headmaster and those teachers present that he had arranged for Badger Watts to enter the Ashton World Conker Championship, as a reward for winning the school tournament. It was a remarkable feat, and had taken a lot of hard talking and persuasion on his part, but somehow he'd managed it. The other members of staff were delighted, although somewhat surprised, with Mr Leaton's achievements, and even Miss Stoat offered her congratulations, suggesting that a cup of coffee was called for. Mr Leaton made his excuses and went off to his classroom. 'Now where were those books that needed marking?' he said to himself.

As Badger and Joey were walking home that afternoon, Joey couldn't help noticing that his friend was strangely quiet. Joey was puzzled because his best pal should have been delighted, perhaps even ecstatic, over the events of the past school day. At the morning's assembly the headmaster had mentioned both of the boys by name. Not only that, but they were each made to stand out at the front while the rest of the children gave them a big clap for taking part in the school conker competition. Whilst Mr North agreed that it was slightly unfortunate that more children didn't attend, both Badger Watts and Joey Roberts took part, and that's what counted. Indeed, as a special reward for their efforts, Mr North had said, he and a number of other teachers had worked *extremely* hard in arranging their prizes, which would be – and here he paused to keep the children in suspense – a special invite for the boys to attend the Ashton World Conker Championships. Badger would be entering the competition and Joey could go along and give him some support. The children in the audience had all said 'Ahhh' and 'Cor' when the headmaster made the announcement, and they immediately told Badger and Joey how lucky they were.

But it was a dejected Badger who walked home that afternoon.

'Ah come on, Badger,' said Joey, trying to cheer his forlorn friend. 'I mean, you're going to enter the world championship. You should be delighted.'

'Yeah, I know,' replied Badger, 'but it's not right, is it? Be honest, I only won one game and my conker never actually hit anything.'

'Yeah, but at least you did win,' Joey enthused, still trying to cheer his friend.'

'What, Miss Take? You heard her say that she'd never actually played conkers before. My granny could have beaten her.'

'Well, she beat me, didn't she?'

'No she didn't. You said yourself that it wasn't fair. No, I think I'll tell Sporty that I can't play.'

'What? Are you barmy? Why do you want to do that? You might even win the world championship.'

'Huh, fat chance. Did you hear Sporty say that I

should use the same conker because it might be a lucky one? Some hopes, it hasn't even had a proper contest yet.'

'Look let's leave it until tonight,' replied Joey, 'and then we'll see if we can think of something to help us for the tournament.'

Next day Joey arrived late at school, his mid-morning dental appointment taking the place of his maths lesson. Joey thought that the dentist's drill was a good swap for long-multiplication sums. Surprisingly, though, he'd chosen to return to school after his appointment, something he'd never done before. His mother was shocked and suggested that it would perhaps be a good idea if they visited the doctor's. However, Joey managed to persuade her that all was well and that he wanted to go and finish off the model of the Viking boat, which had been damaged by someone throwing conkers into it.

The real reason for Joey wanting to return to school was to speak to Badger about an idea he'd had for the tournament. But it wasn't until going home time that he got the chance to speak to his friend. He waited until most of the children had left the room.

'Listen, Badger, I've had a great idea,' said Joey. 'Not only should you enter the World Conker Championship, but I think you can win it!'

'Now it's you who's barmy!' said Badger.

'No, listen. You can win it. All we have to do is be a little dishonest.'

'What do you mean?' said Badger inquisitively.

'Well, let's face it, you haven't got much chance against the other competitors, even if we do use your "lucky" conker,' he added with a touch of sarcasm. ''Cause I read ages ago that some people travel all over the world looking for the perfect nut.'

'So?' said Badger with a totally puzzled look on his face.

'So we use something different. Something that just looks like a conker.'

'Such as?'

'Such as a walnut. Remember when we were down at the market last Saturday and there was that weird-looking bloke on that fruit and veg stall?'

'Oh yeah, him with the mouldy fruit?'

'That's right. Well, he had a pile of nuts, didn't he? All we have to do is find out if he has any walnuts. If he does, we buy some, put a little bit of brown paint on them and use those.'

'Oh yeah, sure,' replied Badger. 'Walnuts look nothing like conkers.'

'Not normally. But a smooth walnut would easily pass for a wrinkled conker, especially if it's painted. And anyway, no one will ever look closely because they won't suspect anything.'

'Well, I hate to tell you this, brain box, but you can break walnuts open quite easily. They're not solid inside.'

'Ah yes, well, I've thought of that as well,' said Joey enthusiastically. 'Our next-door neighbour, Mr Simmonds, is laying a new path in his garden next weekend. Mum's arranged for me to help him so that she can go shopping. She said it will keep me out of mischief.'

'What's that got to do with anything?' asked Badger, who thought he understood Joey's plan up until this point.

'Cor blimey! Are you thick or what?' said Joey.

'Don't you see? All we have to do is saw a walnut in half, fill it with cement and then stick it back together. As long as we remember to thread it onto a lace, it'll work fine. No one will ever know.'

'Hmm. It's a bit dishonest, isn't it?'

'Look,' said Joey, 'even with your best conker, you're not going to win, are you? Not against those other competitors. Some of them are almost professionals.'

'Are you sure no one would notice?' asked Badger, now showing a definite interest in Joey's little plot.

''Course they wouldn't. No one would suspect a thing. It all comes down to deciding if you want to be the World Conker Champion.'

'Well, I wouldn't mind.'

'Well, then. Let's do it!'

'If you're sure no one will find out,' said Badger.

'No chance!'

'Okay. I feel a bit scared, but I'll give it a go.'

'It'll be all right,' said Joey, I'm sure of it.'

'I hope so,' replied Badger. 'I guess I won't be needing this now,' and with that he pulled out of his pocket the shiny brown conker with which he'd won Saturday's tournament. He placed it on the desk nearest to him at the front of the classroom, its black lace, with a small piece of yellow cotton attached to it, hung lazily over the edge of the table.

'Come on, let's go and make our plans,' said Joey, and the two boys headed out of the door.

Ten minutes after the two boys had left, Mr Leaton walked back into the classroom. He'd been delayed by a particularly fussy set of parents who had insisted on knowing whether their daughter Elsie would become a brain surgeon or an astronaut. Secretly, Mr Leaton thought that Elsie was more suited to a career as a full-time daydreamer. But he managed to persuade the parents that they should wait a little longer to see how their daughter progressed. As he entered the room he noticed a conker lying on the desk top next to his own.

'I thought we'd seen the last of these,' he said to himself. He picked the nut up and looked over to the waste-paper basket. He noticed that it had already been emptied by Mr Sponge, so he popped the conker into his jacket pocket, and then turned and headed off home.

5

The following Saturday was once again market day in the town of Grizzleby. This was of no interest to Joey's next door neighbour, Mr Simmonds, who was laying a new concrete path in his garden. He'd also offered to look after Joey whilst the boy's mother went shopping. Mr Simmonds tried hard to teach Joey the skills required to lay a path, but somehow Joey managed to put more of the sand and cement mixture onto his hands and clothes. In fact, he'd also put a great deal onto Mr Simmonds' hands and clothes as well. In addition to this, Joey had planted three snails into the cement – to see if they'd survive – and drawn a smiley face with the words 'Joey was here' written underneath it. Unfortunately, Mr Simmonds had spotted the etched face and inscription when trying to smooth out his dog's footprints. The dog, Rover, had managed to run the whole length of the drying path whilst chasing a small ball that Joey had thrown, telling him to 'fetch'. It was therefore, a very relieved Mr Simmonds who saw Badger walking towards the house.

'Blimey!' said Badger when he saw his friend Joey. 'I thought you were going to put the cement on the path.'

'What do you mean?' asked Joey. 'We have, haven't we, Mr Simmonds?'

'Er, yes well, um,' hesitated the next-door neighbour. 'Well, thanks for your, er, help Joey. Now

I'm sure that you'll want to run along with your friend, Badger. I'm very pleased to see you, Badger. Very, very pleased to see you.'

'Are you sure you can manage without me, Mr Simmonds?' asked Joey, ''Cause I don't mind staying a bit longer.'

'Oh yes, I'm quite sure, thank you. In fact I know that I'll definitely get the job finished now. So off you go. You'd better run home and wash that cement off before it dries.'

'Okay, Mr Simmonds. Come on, Badger, I'll go and clean myself up, and then we'll go down to the market.'

''Bye, Mr Simmonds,' the boys shouted as they walked carefully through the gate to avoid stepping on the drying path.

'Goodbye, boys,' echoed Mr Simmonds, who for the first time that morning began to sing.

'Hey,' said Badger, 'your mum'll go spare when she sees you. You're covered in that stuff.'

'No she won't, 'cause she's not here,' replied Joey.

Well, that's lucky. You're absolutely plastered. Look, there's even some in your hair.'

'That's not all. I've got some here as well, look.'

With that Joey thrust open his trousers pocket. Nestling in his pocket was a wedge of wet cement.

'Ergh, that's disgusting!' complained Badger. 'What do you want that for?'

'What do you think I want it for? You haven't forgotten, have you?'

'No, but I didn't think . . .'

'You never do think, do you?' argued Joey. 'I couldn't stay all squeaky clean, could I? Otherwise Mr Simmonds would have seen a wet patch on my jeans and noticed that I'd got a pocketful of cement.'

'Oh, that wet patch?' said Badger looking at his friend's trousers. 'I thought you'd forgotten to go to the toilet!' he chuckled.

'Very funny,' retorted Joey. 'Anyway, it's worked, hasn't it? 'Cause I got covered in the stuff, he didn't notice this little lot, did he?' and Joey picked a handful of damp crumbly cement from his pocket. 'All we have to do now is put it in a plastic bag to keep it damp, and then it won't go hard. When we've done that we'll hide it in the shed. Mum'll never find it, she hardly ever goes in there.'

'Okay, I'll put the cement in a bag while you go and get washed. We've still got to get down to the market and see if that funny-looking bloke has got any walnuts on his stall.'

Badger searched around for a plastic bag into which he could scoop the wet cement from his friend's discarded jeans.

'So far, so good,' shouted Joey as he bounded up the stairs two at a time.

Down at the market Harry Sprout was once again standing behind his stall of mixed produce. He was sorting through brown cardboard boxes and pulling out small orange-coloured nylon mesh bags. He was muttering to himself under his breath.

'Roll on next week,' he said. 'I need a holiday. This market lark's getting to be too much like hard work, especially when it's as cold as it is today.' Harry was chilled to the bone, hungry and extremely tired. The reason for his tiredness was a delivery late last night. In fact, it was very, very late. By the time that Harry had sorted out just which delivery it was, and checked all the paperwork, it was early morning and time to set up his stall.

'It's not right,' he moaned to himself. 'At least other jobs let you get eight hours' sleep every night. I got twenty minutes, and I still haven't sorted all the stuff out properly. Now where are those wretched walnuts? It's a good job Ed isn't expecting them until next week.'

Harry smiled to himself as he thought how pleasant it would be to sleep from one weekend to the next, but then he had to duck quickly behind a pile of potatoes as he thought he spotted a customer.

'Hello,' said a voice.

'I'm closed, go away.'

'But I only want to say thank you,' an elderly woman's voice replied.

'What? Oh, okay.' Harry stood up.

'Yes, thank you very much for the lovely grapes last week. They were grapes, you know. I had four of them, and my cough's a lot better.'

'Well, thank you, madam. Now I haven't got any more. Try the next stall, I'm very busy.'

'You don't look very busy,' said the woman.

'Yes I am,' Harry replied. 'Look,' he said, pointing to the box of newly arrived walnuts, 'I've got to get this lot sorted out and on display. So I haven't got time to stand and talk.'

'Nor have I,' said the woman. 'I'm busy too, you know. I've got to go and make a doctor's appointment. Anyway, I only wanted to say thank you,' and with that she ambled slowly into the crowd of shoppers.

'Silly old bat,' Harry said to himself. 'Oh well, I might as well finish this lot off,' and he sat down and began sorting the remaining bags of nuts. They were specially selected and packed 12 to a bag.

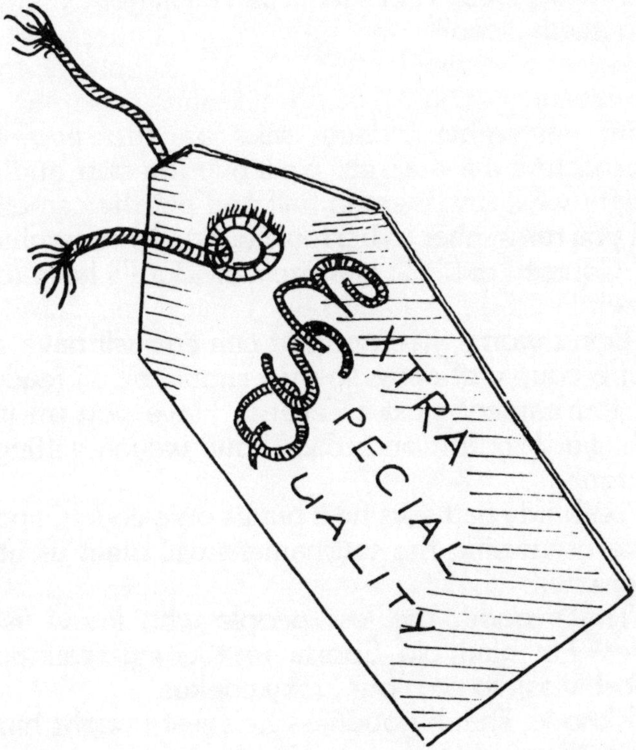

In a short time, he was at the bottom of one of the boxes, and he had a nice display of orange mesh bags piled neatly in front of him on his stall.

'Ha ha,' he said to himself as he picked out the last two bags of nuts from the box. '"Extra Special Quality" the label says. They'll be the ones for Ed.' With that he threw the brown carton onto the pile of rubbish behind him, and then carefully placed the two specially labelled bags behind the rest of the pile. 'I'll put these somewhere safe. Well done, Harry boy, you've just earned yourself a nice little sum of money.

You know, today isn't such a bad day after all. I mean, who needs sleep?'

'Now remember,' Joey said as the two boys approached the market, 'we'll buy the nuts and then tonight we'll saw them in half and put the cement in. Did you remember to borrow your dad's superglue?'

''Course I did,' Badger replied. 'But I'll have to put it back.'

'Don't worry, I reckon the cement will have dried after a couple of days, so they should be all ready for the tournament next weekend. Have you arranged with your mum and dad how we're getting to Ashton?'

'Yeah. My dad says he'll put us on a coach, and the bloke organising the tournament will meet us at the other end.'

'That's good, the less people who know us the better. I'm glad old Sporty isn't going 'cause he'll probably ask to see your *lucky* conker.'

'I know. Thank goodness he's just bought himself that new sports car.'

The boys approached the fresh-produce stall run by Harry Sprout. 'H. Sprout – FRESH FRUIT AND VEGETABLES' the sign beneath the tarpaulin read.

'Hey look, Badger. We're in luck. Look at all those walnuts in those orange bags. There's loads of 'em.'

'All right, but be quick. We don't want anyone to see us,' Badger said nervously.

Joey approached the stall, and failed to spot Harry, who was sitting on a small box using the jagged edge of his front door key to clean the inside of his little fingernail.

'Hello?' Joey shouted into the empty stall. Harry

jumped, narrowly missing jamming the key into his finger.

'Argh! What do you want?' he said, without standing up from behind the pile of potatoes.

'Hey, Joey,' said Badger, who had moved up to stand beside his friend, 'that pile of potatoes just spoke to you!'

Joey began to laugh.

'Shut up, you fool. The bloke's behind them.'

Hearing the voices of the two young boys, Harry Sprout stood up.

'I'll make short work of these,' he said to himself. 'Clear off. I'm closed. You kids shouldn't be allowed around here. You should be at home or locked up somewhere.'

'But we only want to buy some nuts,' said Joey, 'Er, for my granny. She's really ill – she got run over.'

'Hmmph. She should look where she's going, shouldn't she?' Harry Sprout replied unsympathetically.

'But it wasn't her fault, mister,' added Badger. 'It was the bloke who was riding the push-bike.'

'What? She was run over by a bike?'

'Er, yes. That's why we need to cheer her up,' said Joey in an unconvincing voice. It's the shock of it. I've got some money. Look.' He stretched forward a sweaty hand to show Harry the crumpled banknote, revealing five blackened fingernails as he did so.

'Ergh,' thought Harry, and he shivered with revulsion. He quickly regained his composure. 'Oh well,' he said, seeing the chance of some easy money. 'How much have you got?'

'Just this,' replied Joey, still clutching the note. 'How much are those walnuts?'

'Just this!' said Harry, and he snapped his hand

forward and snatched the note from Joey's grubby fingers in less time than it takes to blink an eye. 'But I tell you what, boys,' said Harry generously, 'as they're for your granny, I'll let you have two bags. Walnuts, wasn't it? Help yourself.'

With this he returned to his small wooden box. He perched himself carefully on the edge, and then resumed the delicate task of picking the dirt from his nails with his front door key.

'Come on, quick,' said Joey. 'This bloke's weird. Let's grab a bag each. The bigger and smoother they are the better.' The two boys approached the pile of nuts from the side of the stall. They had each selected a nylon bag, when Badger stopped. He gazed straight ahead.

'Hey look, Joey,' he whispered, and then dug his elbow into his friend's ribs. 'Look at those two bags there. They've got a label on, "Extra Special Quality". They must be really good. Let's have those.'

'All right, but be quick. Grab them before he sees us. He might be keeping those for himself.'

With that, Badger stretched forward and swapped the two labelled bags for the ones they'd previously selected. Checking that they hadn't been seen, the boys turned to leave.

'Thanks, mister,' shouted Joey as they left the stall.

Stupid kids! thought Harry, as he sucked his little finger, which had now started to bleed. It's a good job I know how to handle them.

6

When the boys returned to Joey's house, his mother was not too pleased. She had returned home to find small patches of wet cement on the living room carpet, and she said that the bathroom looked like a builder's yard. Joey told his mother that he was very sorry, but Mr Simmonds must have accidentally spilled some cement on him when he was helping earlier on.

'Well, he should know better,' said Joey's mother. 'After all, he's a grown man. Mind you, it doesn't surprise me. Do you know that when I walked past the path that you helped him to lay, I noticed that he'd cemented three snails into it! How cruel can you get?'

Joey felt himself going red.

'Cor,' Joey said, 'that *is* cruel.'

Badger immediately guessed who had actually carried out this gruesome caper, and he had to cover his face with his handkerchief in order to stop himself laughing. Joey's mum eyed him suspiciously.

'Well, off you go now, boys. Outside and play. I suppose I'll have to clear this mess up.'

The boys hurried out through the back door and into the garden. Each of them had a bag of the recently purchased walnuts tucked into their pocket. Joey checked that his mother wasn't watching them and then he crept over to the garden shed. He lifted the latch, which made a scraping sound as it pushed against the retaining bar.

'Quick,' said Joey, 'in here.'

The boys hurried into the dark, dusty interior of the shed.

'Cor, it's dark!' complained Badger. 'Haven't you got a light?'

''Course we haven't. It's a garden shed, isn't it? Anyway, we haven't used it since Dad left home. You'll be able to see when your eyes get used to it.'

Sure enough, Badger found that his eyes did gradually adjust to the dim interior of the shed, and after a few minutes the small amount of light coming in through the cobweb-covered window appeared more than adequate.

'Right,' said Joey, 'find a saw!'

After a brief search Joey had found himself a small hacksaw, whilst Badger, after upturning a box full of old flowerpots, had discovered a small tenon saw. He said that it reminded him of a mass murderer in a horror film that he recently watched on a home video. Joey shivered at the thought and told his pal to be quiet. Suitably armed, the boys set to work. They each opened a bag of the precious walnuts and, trying to hold them steady with one hand, they began to saw.

'Try and saw across the middle. If you look, there's a sort of ridge running around them,' Joey instructed.

'I know,' replied Badger, 'but it's hard, isn't it? I didn't think that it would be this difficult.'

'You can't expect to be World Conker Champion without a bit of hard work,' Joey admonished.

The boys worked enthusiastically at trying to saw the walnuts in half, but they had little success. Holding the nuts and sawing them was nearly impossible. All that Joey had succeeded in doing was making a large groove in his middle finger, causing it to bleed profusely. It was only when Badger spotted the vice attached to the edge of the workbench that they had any success. He immediately placed a walnut between the two faces of the rusty green machine and turned the bar, tightening the wooden blocks against the nut, holding it firmly in place.

'Great stuff!' said Joey. 'Now we'll really get going.'

Badger started to saw, and to his surprise a deep groove began to appear in the nut as the small hand-held saw did its work.

'You carry on, I'll go and fetch the cement,' instructed Joey.

'Hey, Joey,' Badger called out, 'there's weird plastic-looking stuff on the outside of this nut. It follows the line that I'm sawing down.'

'Is there? I expect it grew like that. Remember they're special quality nuts. That's what the labels say. Anyway, don't bother about it now because we've got twenty-four to saw in half.'

'What? are we doing them all?' asked Badger.

'Well, we'll do what we can,' Joey replied. 'But however many we do we'll have to be quick because we've got to use the cement before it dries.'

With that, Joey carefully opened the shed door and peered out to check that his mother wasn't in the garden.

'I'll be back in a minute,' he said, and went out into the bright sunlit garden.

In the dim light of the shed Badger continued to work enthusiastically, attacking each of the walnuts with his saw.

'The mad saw-man creeps up on another nut!' he said to himself. 'Oh save me! Save me!' he continued in a high-pitched voice. 'Too late, nut!' and he gave a small scream as the nut dropped into two halves onto the shed floor.

In the murky setting of his horror film, and in his haste to cut as many nuts as possible, Badger failed to notice that with each movement of the saw, a fine white powder fell effortlessly from the nut. The brilliant white powder was mixing with the dust created by sawing the walnut. It fell to the murky depths of the wooden floor, hidden amongst the dirt and dust that had gathered over the past years.

'How many have you done?' asked Joey as he reappeared at the door carrying a plastic bag containing the cement.

'You took your time. Where've you been?' replied Badger, ignoring his friend's question.

'Yeah, I know. I'm sorry but Mum wanted to know what I was doing. Anyway, I've got to go out with her in half an hour, so we'll have to stop sawing and start sticking. So how many have you done?'

Badger had a quick count up of the empty half-shells that were lying clustered together on the top of the workbench.

'Twelve,' he said. 'That's exactly half of them.'

'Well, that's more than enough,' replied Joey. 'Let's put the cement in them and stick them together.'

'Yeah, okay. But there's something funny about these walnuts,' continued Badger, ''cause I haven't found any nuts inside. They're all clean, empty shells.'

'What do you mean, "no nuts inside"?' questioned Joey. 'You're sawing the nuts.'

'No. I mean the part that you eat, the bit in the middle. The kernel or something it's called. I remember it from one of Sporty's science lessons.'

'Well, I expect you cut it into little bits when you sawed through the nut,' answered Joey, not really sure what Badger was talking about. 'Anyway, it doesn't matter, we only need the shells. Here.'

Joey held up the plastic bag and placed it on the bench, In the secrecy of the garden shed the boys began to fill the walnut cases with the wet cement.

'Here's the glue,' said Badger, producing a small black and white tube from his pocket. 'Don't get it on your fingers or it won't come off.'

'I'm not stupid,' replied Joey.

The boys worked feverishly at their task and very soon 12 cement-filled walnuts were lying motionless on the workbench.

'Right,' said Joey, 'let's put all of these in one bag, and those we haven't done in the other bag. Take the label off so that we know which bag is which.'

'Okay,' said Badger, and he emptied out the unprepared nuts. 'Are you sure you haven't done these?' he asked. 'They look like there's a line of glue around them.'

''Course I haven't,' replied Joey. 'Come on, my mum'll be wondering where I am.'

'Arrrgh!' screamed Badger, just as he'd finished filling the two bags. 'You know what we haven't done, don't you?' he said in a desperate voice. 'We haven't threaded the laces.'

'Oh no!' gasped Joey. 'Why didn't you say so earlier?'

'Well, I didn't know, did I? Anyway, I wasn't going to get the laces.'

The boys began to argue, but Joey realised that he should have been ready to go out with his mum ages ago.

'Don't worry,' he said. 'It's too late to do anything about it now anyway because the glue will have dried.' He paused, 'I know. We'll drill a hole through them and then thread them onto a lace. We've got a drill.'

'Oh great,' replied Badger. 'We're engineers now!'

'No, it's easy. It'll look more realistic anyway. We'll do it tomorrow night 'cause my mum will be out. She's working down at the club. Come on, I've got to go, she'll go barmy. Don't worry, we'll still be at the tournament on Saturday.'

'Oh boy!' Badger said to himself, hiding the two mesh bags beneath a pile of old newspapers in the bottom of an old box. After making sure that the nuts were safely hidden away, the two boys quickly arranged to meet the following evening. Having done this they slipped quietly out of the shed.

The following evening the boys met up as previously arranged. Badger arrived at his friend's house immediately after tea. Joey's mother had already left for her evening job, working as a barmaid.

'Is your mum here?' asked Badger as soon as his friend opened the door.

'No, she's out, so we can get started. Look, I've even found some paint,' Joey replied.

Badger entered the sparsely decorated living room.

'Are you sure that this will work?' he asked.

'Of course it will,' Joey replied. 'Look, I'll fetch the drill down from upstairs. I know where Mum hides it. You go and fetch the walnuts from the shed.'

Joey disappeared up the stairs, whilst Badger headed towards the back door. He turned the key and stepped out into the garden. After a few seconds, and a brief struggle with the latch, Badger stepped into the murky interior of the garden shed. He pulled out the brown cardboard box from beneath the bench and lifted the dusty newspapers that were lying inside.

Two nylon bags, each containing 12 walnuts, were lying in exactly the same position as he had placed them the previous evening. Each bag still had a bright red label attached to it.

'Oh no!' cried Badger, 'I forgot to take the label off the bag of nuts that we'd cemented. Now I don't know which bag is which.'

He snatched a walnut from one of the bags in order to check it. There was a fine line of solidified glue clearly visible around the nut.

'These must be the ones,' he said to himself. However, as he picked up a walnut from the other bag, he noticed that there was also a line of clear dried liquid around it. 'Oh no! This one looks exactly the same. In fact they all do,' he said, glancing at the other nuts.

'Are you coming or what?'

Badger jumped.

'Cor, you didn't half frighten me,' said Badger, realising it was his pal Joey coming to see where he was.

'Well, come on. We haven't got all night,' Joey ordered.

Badger grabbed one of the orange nylon bags and marched quickly out of the shed and back towards the house.

Although the drilling of the walnuts was a difficult operation – mainly because the electric drill was so heavy – the boys managed to bore through all 12 nuts in remarkably quick time. They took turns at drilling, with one boy holding the nut steady in a pair of nutcrackers, and the other operating the drill. Admittedly they had made a couple of small holes in the kitchen table when Joey pressed too hard with the drill but this apart, both boys were quite pleased with how simple the task had been.

'I thought drilling through cement would have been harder than that,' said Badger as he brushed up the white dusty powder with his hands.

'I didn't,' Joey replied, as he threaded the walnuts onto an assortment of laces. 'Not with an electric drill. Mind you, it looks as if some of the cement has turned to powder because it keeps falling out of the holes that we drilled. Perhaps some of it got too dry. Anyway,' he added as he blew some of the white dust from the table, 'it shouldn't affect the walnuts. Or

should I say conkers? They'll be solid enough. You'll see.'

By the end of the evening the two boys stood back and admired their work. On the table in front of them lay 12 sparkling conkers, or to be more precise, 12 filled walnuts. Each was threaded onto a bootlace and painted a deep brown colour. Apart, that is, from a small circular area at the top of the nut which was left as it was – a light shade of yellow brown.

'I think we're ready for the World Conker Tournament,' said Joey. 'Just think, Badger, this Saturday you'll be the World Conker Champion.'

Badger nervously gathered up the conkers and put them in the orange nylon bag.

'You know,' he said, 'I think this might work after all.'

7

For a third consecutive Saturday Harry Sprout stood behind his market stall trying to look as if he was interested in selling his produce. Whether he did sell anything or not didn't really matter – especially this weekend. Ed Stone would soon be along to pick up his special delivery of walnuts, which meant that Harry would also be getting a nice little roll of banknotes. This thought, along with the fact that Harry was having a half-day off today, had put him in an exceedingly good mood. Indeed, at one point he'd even thought of giving some free samples of his fruit and veg to anyone who showed an interest in his stall. Unfortunately, most of the market customers had now seen the quality of Harry's produce and gave his overripe fruit and wrinkled vegetables a wide berth. After 20 minutes waiting for an interested customer, Harry eventually gave up and went back to muttering rude comments about the shoppers.

'I wish Ed would hurry up,' he moaned. 'Then I can clear off home. I've got a long way to go this afternoon.' He kicked a mouldy orange from beneath his stall, which rolled out amongst the shoppers.

'I shouldn't go kicking fruit about like that if I were you,' said a voice.

Harry, startled, looked up in front of him.

'Ed!' he shouted. 'Good to see you again.'

'Ssshhh, you fool,' whispered Ed, looking around him. 'You're not supposed to know me.'

'Ooops. Oh yeah sorry, Ed.' Harry composed himself. 'Ah, good morning sir,' he shouted in a loud voice, hoping that any passers-by might hear. 'Can I help you at all, sir? We have some lovely fresh vegetables.'

At this point the man on the next stall began to cough and splutter. Harry looked across and gave him a fierce glare.

'Good morning. Do you have any walnuts? I just fancy some, you know. Only the best quality, mind.' Ed spoke quickly and nervously. He appeared to want to get the purchase over as quickly as possible.

'Ah yes, sir,' replied Harry, over-acting. 'I've got some here.' He bent down behind him and reached into a large cardboard box. 'All my walnuts arrived last week, sir, and I selected two bags especially for you. I kept them separate from the others. Special quality these are, you know.'

'Splendid!' Ed replied.

Harry lifted out a small plastic bag containing the two nylon sacks of walnuts that he thought he'd kept separate from last week's delivery.

'Here you are, sir!' said Harry, handing over the bag.

'Thanks,' Ed Stone replied. 'Er, I think you'll find enough here to pay for the nuts,' and he very quickly slipped an envelope into Harry's hand. Harry glanced down and saw a huge stack of banknotes beneath the open flap of the brown Inland Revenue envelope.

'Blimey,' Harry said to himself, and looked up at Ed, who was examining one of the nylon mesh bags. Ed's face became agitated, and he quickly pulled out the second orange bag.

'You bungling buffoon!' cried Ed. 'These aren't the ones. I wanted the special walnuts. The bags with the red labels on.' His face began to turn a deep purple colour and his small shifty eyes began to bulge and pulsate as his voice got louder.

'But they have got red labels on,' Harry replied, 'look . . .' and he snatched one of the bags from Ed.

'Oo'er,' said Harry. 'If I get a hundred years in prison I'll never speak to you again, and I'll never sell you anything from my stall either.'

'Just shut up and find those walnuts!' ordered Ed.

'Oh why did we have to lose them today? Today of all days,' moaned Harry. 'I'm supposed to be going out this afternoon.'

'You won't be going anywhere *ever* again if you don't get me those nuts. Think, man. Where did you put them?'

Harry racked his brains and tried to remember. He squeezed his hand underneath a box of overripe Seville oranges that were on display.

'Ahhh!' he shouted.

'What? Have you found them?' Ed gasped, springing forward.

'No, look. A spider!' said Harry as he backed away from the eight-legged arthropod. He'd never liked spiders. Not since he'd found one in his lunch box beneath his peanut butter sandwich.

Ed gnashed his teeth.

'Why did I ever let myself work with this idiot,' he said to himself.

The two men continued to hunt amongst the discoloured produce lazily arranged on Harry's stall, scattering the goods as they did so. Finally, after a frantic half an hour, they both sat in a state of total exhaustion.

'Well, they're not here,' remarked Harry. 'Now what do we do?'

'We *must* find them. Can't you think where you put them?'

Harry sat and thought. But the harder he tried the less he remembered. In fact, all he could think of was the fact that he should be going out this afternoon and he was already late.

'Look, Ed,' he said, as the two men sat behind the stall. 'I'm all excited about my trip this afternoon. That's all I can think about. If I was calm and relaxed I might remember where I put the walnuts. Let me go and have my afternoon off, I'm sure it will help.'

Ed sat in silence, pondering the thought.

'All right,' he said, but I'm coming with you.'

'What?' replied Harry. 'Why?'

'Because I want to be there when you do remember. Anyway, how am I to know that you haven't kept them for yourself?'

'Ahhh Ed, that's mean,' answered Harry.

'Yes it is,' replied Ed calmly. 'And I'm going to be a lot meaner if you don't remember what you did with those nuts. Now come on, let's get off to wherever it is we're going.'

'Well, we'll have to take a taxi now, 'cause we're late.' replied Harry sulkily.

'Where is it then?'

'It's a small place called Ashton,' answered Harry as they set off to find a taxi.

8

Badger and Joey had arrived at Ashton well before the tournament was due to start, and so far their plans had gone without a hitch. Badger's father had ensured that they were both safely on the coach before he set off for his morning shift. Then the organiser of the competition, Colonel Filbert, had met the boys as arranged, when the bus arrived in the small Northamptonshire village. Badger had his orange bag of conker lookalikes hidden safely away in his sports bag, and as yet no one had asked any awkward questions. Despite this, both boys felt extremely nervous as they sat eating the beefburger that Colonel Filbert had bought for each of them.

'How long before we start?' asked Badger.

'You asked me that two minutes ago,' replied Joey.

'Well, how long is there?'

'About twenty minutes,' Joey answered. 'Don't worry. You'll be all right. Try not to get nervous.'

'I'm n-not n-nervous,' Badger replied.

'You're not?'

'No. I'm terrified! I just want to get this over with as quickly as possible. I didn't think that there'd be this many people here. Did you see that TV camera as we came in?'

Joey began to cough and splutter.

'Oh no!' he gasped, choking on a small piece of barbecued beef.

'What's up? Are you all right?' asked Badger.

'I was,' replied Joey. 'But you know you just mentioned about a lot of people being here?' he gasped between coughs. He paused to take a mouthful of cola from a paper cup.

'Yes. What about it?'

'Well, you know one of them. Look, over there, coming towards us.'

'Oh no!' cried Badger. 'I didn't think he was coming.'

'Neither did I,' replied Joey.

'Hello, boys. How are we today? All set?'

'H-h-hello, Mr Leaton,' the shocked boys replied.

'Oh dear. You sound quite jumpy, boys. Oh well, I quite understand. I expect that you're nervous. I thought I'd come along and cheer you on, Badger. Lend a bit of support and all that.'

'Oh . . . er thanks, Sport – er, Mr Leaton,' replied Badger, sounding totally unimpressed.

'I thought you'd be out in your new sports car today, Mr Leaton,' Joey said to his teacher.

'Ah yes, well er, my erm, friend who I normally drive with she, er he, didn't want to go out today,' Sporty replied.

'So are you by yourself then, Mr Leaton?' continued Joey inquisitively.

'Erm yes, I am for now. Say, how's that lucky conker of yours, Badger? All polished and ready?' Mr Leaton asked, trying to avoid any more of Joey's awkward questions.

'Er yes, thank you, Mr Leaton,' said Badger.

'But you can't see it,' Joey added immediately his friend had finished speaking.

'Why on earth would I want to see it?' asked Mr Leaton.

'Er, just in case you did. It's bad luck,' added Joey. 'Isn't it, Badger?' and he gave his friend a quick tap on the ankle with his shoe.

'Ouch! Er, yes it is, Mr Leaton. I never get my conkers out before a tournament. It's well known that it brings bad luck,' Badger confirmed.

'Well I never,' said Sporty. 'I've been playing conkers ever since I was your age, and I never knew that. Perhaps that's why I never won any tournaments, eh boys?' and he laughed at his own suggestion.

The boys were rescued by a voice on the tannoy.

'Would the eight competitors for the World Conker Championship please make their way to the centre of the recreation ground,' the posh voice said.

'Eight?' asked Badger.

'Yes, that's right,' replied Mr Leaton, unbuttoning his jacket. 'There's only eight entrants this year. Apparently quite a few contestants have pulled out, it's been such a bad year for conkers. That's why *you're* extremely lucky to be able to enter. Come on. Let's go and see who you're playing.'

The boys strolled slowly over to where a large crowd had gathered. As they did so, Badger noticed two tall black policemen's helmets.

'What are they doing here?' he asked nervously. 'What do they want?'

'Oh those. I expect they're on crowd control duty,' Mr Leaton replied. 'Anyway, I wouldn't worry about them, they're not here to arrest you.'

If only you knew, thought Badger, and he glanced quickly across to Joey , who was looking decidedly off colour.

'Will you hurry up?' Harry Sprout said to the taxi

driver. 'I was supposed to be there ten minutes ago!'

'I'm not allowed to go faster then forty miles an hour on this road,' the driver replied.

'Well, go on another road,' snapped Harry.

'No, I always take my passengers on the shortest route. It helps to keep the fare down.'

'I don't care about the fare, just get me to Ashton. It's urgent.'

'You leave this to me, Harry,' interrupted Ed. 'Now listen here, my man,' he said in a smooth voice. 'My friend has to remain as calm and as relaxed as possible. Furthermore, he has to be at this . . . this place in the shortest possible time, so could you please hurry?'

'Well sir,' replied the driver, 'as you know, the

customer is always right, but I still can't break the speed limit. It's against the law.'

'There's a fifty-pound note in my hand,' said Ed, holding a crisp new banknote in front of the driver's eyes.

'I'll get you there in a jiffy!' the driver replied, snatching the note away.

Ed and Harry were forced back into their seats as the car accelerated forward.

'Why do we have to get to this place, Harry? What's so important about it?' inquired Ed.

'Ah well, I'm going to achieve an ambition. It's something I've always wanted to do.

'What's that then? Deliver some goods on time? Ha ha,' and Ed gave an exaggerated sarcastic laugh at his own little joke.

'No, don't be daft,' replied Harry. 'I'm playing conkers!'

'What?' boomed Ed. 'Conkers?'

'Yeah. I knew you'd be pleased. Except if we don't hurry I'll never get there on time.'

Ed's face had turned a deep beetroot-red colour, and he looked as if he was about to explode.

'You mean to tell me that I've lost thousands of pounds worth of valuable goods, and you want to nip off and play conkers?'

'Yeah. Playing conkers helps me to relax.'

Ed immediately lowered his voice and regained his composure.

'Ah yes. Relax. That's a good idea.'

'Yeah. I thought so too,' said Harry. 'You see, if I'm relaxed I might remember where I put those dru – er, walnuts. Hey Ed, do you want to see my best conker? It's a twelver. I'm using it today.'

'Not just now, Harry,' Ed sighed. 'Not just now,'

and he sat back in his seat with a look of total frustration on his face.

9

Harry Sprout and Ed Stone eventually arrived at the small village of Ashton just in time. The loudspeakers were making a final appeal for Mr H Sprout to enter the competition arena. In fact, had Harry been timed to play in either of the first two matches he would have been eliminated because both of these games had already been completed.

Harry dashed over to the referee and announced his presence, whilst Ed used Harry's money to pay for the taxi. Harry needed little preparation time. Whilst he may have been almost totally useless at selling fruit and vegetables, he was an accomplished conker player. A fact noted by his young, narrow-faced opponent, whose nut was soon smashed into tiny little pieces.

The crowd applauded as the winner was announced and even Harry was surprised when Ed rushed over to him.

'Have you remembered? Have you remembered?'

'Remembered what?' replied Harry.

'The nuts, man, the nuts.'

'Oh those. No, not yet. But I'm feeling a lot better. It'll come back to me soon. I'm sure it will.'

'Urr,' sighed Ed.

The announcer stepped forward and requested the presence of the next two competitors. It was Badger's turn.

'Go on, Badger,' said Mr Leaton. 'Show 'em what you're made of.'

I know what my conker's made of, thought Badger. He was in a terrible state. What if anyone spotted that his conkers were fake? What if the TV cameras showed a close-up of his conker? Oh, why did he ever agree to this? It's all right for Joey, he's safely hidden away in the audience.

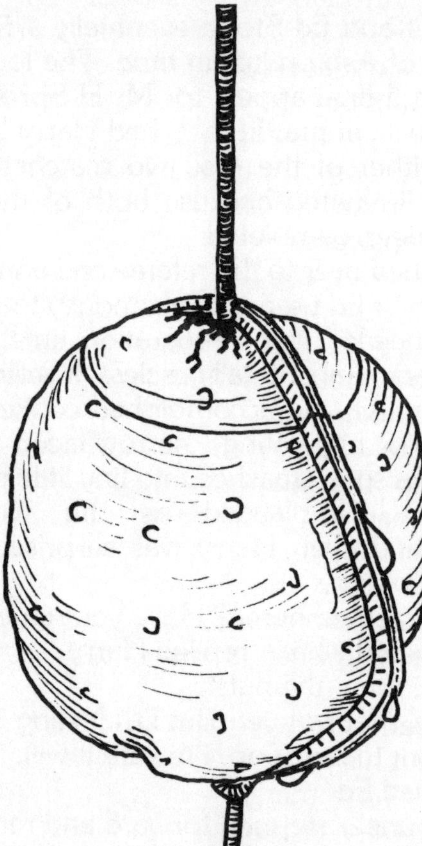

'Come on, Badger,' Mr Leaton encouraged him. 'Don't be nervous,' and he pushed the hesitating child forward.

The crowd had now grown extremely large and was gathered tightly around the small slightly raised platform on which the competition was taking place. Badger was introduced to his opponent, an elderly Rumanian woman who had just three front teeth, one of which stuck out at an obscure angle.

'Hel–hello,' said Badger, clutching the blue sports bag that contained his conkers.

'Vello,' the woman replied. 'View are okay, yes?' she asked in broken English.

'Er, fine,' answered Badger. 'a little n-n-nervous.'

'Could we get started please, sir,' said Police Constable Crotchett, who was on crowd control duty. 'There's quite a lot of people waiting,' and he and his colleague stood behind the young schoolboy, waiting for the action to begin.

Unfortunately for Badger and Joey, as they stepped onto the platform they were spotted by Harry, who had just finished convincing Ed that he was feeling a lot better and far more relaxed.

That's odd, Harry thought to himself. Where have I seen those two before? He racked his brains. He was positive that he'd seen them in the past couple of weeks.

Badger leaned forward and reached down into his bag to pull out his orange sack of false conkers.

'Cor, look how many he's got in there,' said PC Quaver, looking over Badger's shoulder.

'They look a bit dusty to me,' replied PC Crotchett, noticing a fine powder on the nut that Badger had selected. Both policemen had now removed their helmets to avoid blocking the view of the crowds behind them.

In his nervous state, Badger had not only forgotten to select and clean a suitable conker from his bag of nuts, but he'd also forgotten to remove the bright red label which proclaimed 'Extra Special Quality' for all to see. With his shaking hands he pulled out a threaded walnut and held it out at arm's length. He would let his opponent have the first hit in order to get this over with as quickly as possible. In his other hand Badger clutched the bright orange mesh bag, with the bright red label flapping in the wind. It was this that Harry Sprout spotted.

'That's it!' shouted Harry, slapping Ed on the shoulder. 'Look!'

Ed's eyes immediately latched onto the fluttering red label.

'Quick, get that bag,' he ordered. The two men began pushing through the crowd in order to reach Badger on the other side of the playing square.

'I remember now. I know what must have happened.' shouted Harry, heaving and shoving through the packed audience.

'Shut up and get that bag!' exclaimed Ed as he followed on behind. Although they had lost sight of the boys in amongst the crowd, Harry and Ed had now almost reached the part of the platform where Badger and Joey were standing.

'Play,' ordered the referee.

The Rumanian woman's conker stood upright on the end of its string, defying the law of gravity. Then, with the speed of an express train it crashed against Badger's walnut. The fake nut, which now contained only a little of the white powdered drug – since most had fallen out during the delicate drilling operation – instantly exploded into hundreds of tiny pieces, its hollow shell proving no match for the solid horse chestnut. A fine cloud of white powder began to fall onto the floor.

'Just a minute,' said PC Crotchett, noticing the white particles. 'This looks like a very suspicious substance to me. Do all of these *conkers* belong to you?' he asked, pointing to the orange bag that Badger held in his hand.

At that precise moment, Harry pushed through to the front of the crowd where Badger was standing. Harry snatched the bag from Badger's hand.

'Got 'em! These are ours,' he said.

'Are you sure, sir?' said PC Crotchett.

'Absolutely sure. Well, they're his,' replied Harry,

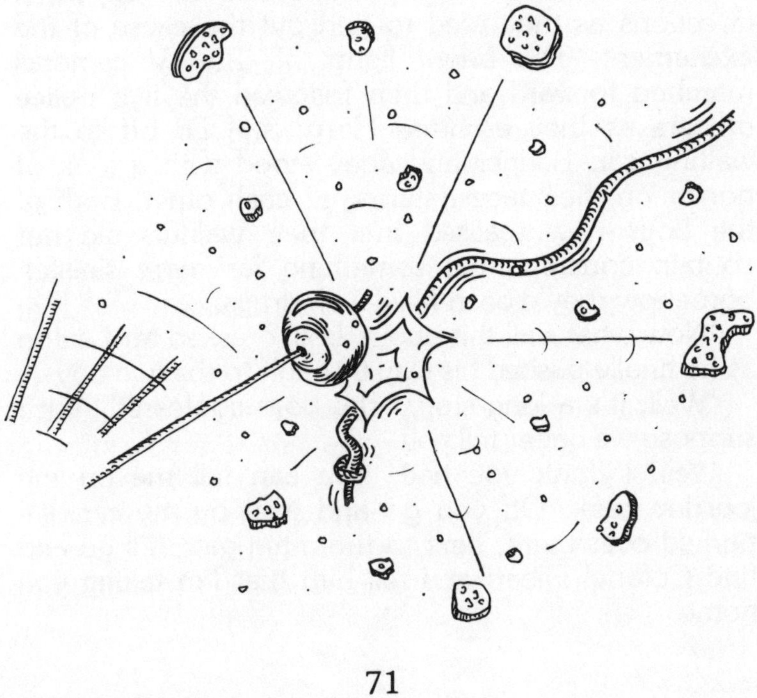

handing the bag to Ed. 'They're nothing to do with these kids. I don't know how they got them. They're ours, all ours, completely, utterly and totally ours. So there!'

'In that case, sir,' said PC Crotchett, putting on his helmet, 'I'd like a word with you. We're police officers.'

'Oo'er,' said Harry.

'I think there's something suspicious about these conkers, which means that you're nabbed,' continued PC Crotchett, slapping a pair of handcuffs onto Harry's wrist.

'So are you,' echoed PC Quaver, and he clicked a pair of equally impressive silver 'cuffs onto Ed's wrist.

For a moment there was total confusion, and everyone seemed to be pushing and shoving in all directions as they tried to find out the cause of the excitement. The bright lights of the TV cameras marched forward and then followed the two police officers as they escorted Harry and Ed off to the waiting car. Badger and Joey stood with a look of horror on their faces, staring at each other. Both of the boys now realised that their walnuts did not contain concrete, but something far more sinister. Somehow they'd been filled with drugs.

'Now what's all this about, boys?' asked Mr Leaton as he finally pushed his way through to the two boys.

'Well, it's a long story,' the boys confessed, 'but I suppose we better tell you.'

'Yes, I think you had. You can tell me on the journey back. Off you go and wait by my car. It's parked over there, next to the main gate. I'll go and find Colonel Filbert and tell him that I'm taking you home.'

The two boys trudged dejectedly off to the main entrance while Sporty Leaton went in search of the competition organiser, Colonel Filbert.

10

After a short break, order was restored and the competition was ready to resume. The first of the two semi-finals was about to begin although there was a slight problem with the second fixture, mainly because one of the players – Harry Sprout – had been arrested and marched off to the police station. Thus, there didn't appear to be anyone available to make up the second semi-final. This fact was causing the competition organiser, Colonel Filbert, a great deal of concern as he stood in a tent next to the stage.

'What am I going to do?' he wailed to his wife Hazel, who was trying to comfort him.

'Don't worry,' she said, 'we'll tell everyone to go home. We'll just call the tournament off.'

'Call the tournament off!' the Colonel roared. 'There are over one thousand people out there. There are national newspapers, radio reporters and TV cameras. There's even a representative of the government, and don't forget those lunatics from the FHC!'

'The FHC?' his wife questioned.

'Yes. The Friends of the Horse Chestnut. They're here to ensure that there isn't any cruelty to horse chestnut trees.'

'Well, horse chestnuts are beautiful trees,' his wife said. 'They do need protecting. It's very important.'

'Oh, please try to be helpful,' the Colonel said. 'I do not need a lecture on the environment,' he added, in a state of total panic.

'Er, excuse me,' said Mr Leaton, having finally located the Colonel.

'Go away please,' replied the Colonel, 'we are extremely busy.'

Mr Leaton tried again.

'But I need –'

'The lavatory? Out of the door, turn right,' the Colonel interrupted. 'Why don't these people read the signs?' he said to himself.

'No!' Mr Leaton answered firmly. 'Please listen, Colonel. I am the teacher of the two boys you met off the coach this morning.'

'Children? Oh, children. Goodness me. I'd forgotten about them,' the Colonel added. 'Where are they?'

'Don't worry,' said Mr Leaton, 'because I'm taking them home.'

'Oh good. Thank you. Well done. For a moment I thought I'd got another problem.'

'Another problem?' asked Mr Leaton. 'Anything I can help with? I seem to have been solving lots of problems lately.'

Colonel Filbert looked at his watch. The first semi-final would be over by now. The second one was due to start any moment, and he still needed a competitor. He quickly explained the problem to the teacher.

'Oh dear!' said Sporty. 'That is a problem. I can't help you with that one, I'm afraid. Still, I must get the boys back to their homes.' He reached into his jacket pocket for his car keys. 'What's this?' he said, and pulled out a long black bootlace which had a shiny brown conker neatly knotted onto its end. 'What on earth. . . ?' gasped Sporty.

'What's that?' stuttered the Colonel.

'It's . . . it's . . . it's a conker!' exclaimed the

surprised teacher.

'I know it's a conker! Where did you get it from?' replied the Colonel.

'I think it's one of the conkers from the school competition. Yes, I remember now. I picked it up from one of the desks in the classroom a day or so after the tournament. I remember putting it into my pocket.'

'You mean this conker has previously entered a tournament?' asked the Colonel.

'Yes, at least it probably has. I'm not sure.'

'It'll do,' the Colonel said. 'Quick, there's no time to lose. Outside and onto the stage. You're our semi-finalist.'

'But, but –'

'There's no time to argue,' the Colonel said. 'If I remember correctly, you'll be playing against the Rumanian woman, Elsie Isitova. Come along now, Mr Leaton.' A delighted Colonel Filbert grasped Sporty Leaton's arm and dragged him out through the tent and onto the raised platform. After a brief word with the officials, Colonel Filbert took over the microphone and explained to the watching crowd how Mr Leaton had very kindly entered his prize conker in order to help the organisers of the competition complete this years semi-finals. 'A particularly noble gesture after the earlier er . . . problems,' the Colonel had said. The crowd cheered as Arthur Leaton was ushered forward to meet his opponent. He found himself standing face to face with the Rumanian lady who a short time ago had wrecked Badger's dreams of becoming World Conker Champion. The two competitors shook hands and then tossed a coin to see who would have first strike.

As it happened the contest only lasted for one hit,

as Mr Leaton's shiny brown weapon shattered the elderly woman's nut into small pieces. This was not because the teacher was a skilled conker player, but was due to the fact that the Rumanian's chestnut had passed through the cloud of deadly white dust in its previous match. The dangerous powdered drug had begun to eat away and rot her conker long before she stepped onto the stage to face Sporty Leaton. Loud cheers rang around the village green as the winner's name was announced over the tannoy. Arthur Leaton was in the final of the World Conker Championship.

Badger and Joey had been standing by the main gate, waiting for their tutor to take them back to their homes. They were both shocked when they heard their teacher's name over the loudspeaker.

'How on earth did that happen?' asked Joey.

'I don't know,' replied Badger, 'but let's go and cheer him on.'

The two boys turned and ran back into the arena to watch the grand final.

The two competitors for the deciding match of the World Conker Championship stood alongside each other as they were introduced to the enthralled crowd. Arthur Leaton, secretly known as Sporty, stood to the right of the stage. He held in his hand a conker which he'd found on a desk a couple of weeks earlier, and he had absolutely no idea who it belonged to. His opponent, standing to his left, was a tall thin Scottish gentleman by the name of Hamish McBiff, otherwise known as Boffer. His conker was specially selected from a group of hand-picked chestnuts that had been individually polished with beeswax and carefully sprayed with a fine mist of Scottish spring water. The two men stood with nervous fixed grins on their faces as newspaper photographers' flashbulbs and TV cameras moved in to obtain close-ups of the men's sweating brows. It was time to begin.

Badger and Joey sat nervously at the side of the stage, watching their teacher, who looked down and smiled at them. Hamish McBiff had the first hit. There was a loud crack as his conker made a solid contact with Sporty's nut. After two or three blows from each chestnut the result was in the balance, with the conker competition swinging in one direction and then the other. A small jagged crack appeared on the outside of McBiff's nut as Mr Leaton's conker made contact. McBiff made his reply, and there was a tangle of

GRAND FINAL!

strings. Joey jumped to his feet.

'No stamps!' he shouted. 'No stamps!'

'Sit down, you twit!' said Badger. 'This is the world championship. People don't go around stamping on each other's conkers.'

'Well, Miss Take stamped on mine.'

'She's not exactly world championship material, is she?' argued Badger. 'She didn't even win the school competition.'

'Nor did Sporty Leaton,' added Joey, 'and look where he is now.'

The boys' conversation was halted as they watched Hamish McBiff unleash a double-arm super swing and thump his conker hard into Mr Leaton's chestnut. There was a loud crack as the nuts collided, and suddenly two halves of a conker shot out at right angles to the hanging string. Both competitors looked down at their laces. A look of horror appeared on Boffer's face. He had slammed his conker so hard against his rival's that this own nut had broken clean in half. Arthur Leaton was conker champion of the world! The audience cheered and the two boys ran forward to offer their congratulations.

The celebrations after the tournament were quite short and involved only a few photographs and a short interview for television and radio. In any case, Mr Leaton couldn't stay long as he had to get the two young lads back to their parents. They were already far too late. In fact, Mr Leaton even refused to answer an urgent telephone call from an attractive young lady called Rosalind, who had just seen his picture on the television. Sporty had decided that it was time to leave without any further delays.

As the two boys and the world champion headed back towards the car park, Badger asked his teacher where he had got his conker from.

'Oh, I found it on the top of a desk in the classroom,' answered Sporty. 'I don't know whose it was, but there's a small piece of yellow cotton tied around the end of the lace. Whoever it belonged to, I hope they didn't mind me using it. I'm afraid it's got a bit of a crack in it now,' and he held the conker up for the boys to see.

'But that was – ouch!' cried Badger, as Joey gave him a sharp dig in the ribs with his elbow.

'I mean,' continued Mr Leaton, 'Just think, someone left a conker lying around that turned out to be a world champion. Fancy that.'

Badger glared at his pal, and thought what might have happened had they stuck to the rules.

'Why did I ever listen to you?' Badger whispered to his friend as they edged ahead of their teacher.

'Well, it was only an idea,' he answered. 'You didn't have to listen to me. I mean, I didn't really want to cheat.'

'Right then, boys,' said Mr Leaton as they reached the car. 'You said that you had some explaining to do on the journey home. But before you do, I really must say, Badger, that I thought your lucky conker would have done better in this competition. Still, some things you can never be sure about, can you, boys?'

'No,' the boys replied in unison.

'You certainly can't!' added Badger with a fierce glare at Joey.

'Now,' said the teacher, revving the car engine, 'what's all this explaining you're going to do?'

'Oh heck,' said Badger to his pal. 'This is going to be a long journey. A *very* long journey.'